SURVIVING THE MONETARY CRASH

Strategies for Surviving a Depression and Monetary Collapse

RENE MULBERY

CONTENTS

DEDICATION

To all those who are trying to survive a Depression and Monetary Collapse, this message is for you.

We know that these are tough times, and the road ahead may seem daunting. But we want you to know that you are not alone. There are millions of people all over the world who are facing similar challenges, and we are all in this together.

We also want you to know that there is hope. With the right strategies and mindset, you can overcome any obstacle that comes your way. By developing self-sustaining practices, building community resilience, and using renewable energy sources, you can create a more sustainable and resilient future for yourself and those around you.

It may not be easy, and there will be days when it wants to give up as the only option. But remember, every challenge is an opportunity to gain experience and become stronger. And every small step you take towards survival and resilience is a victory.

So, to all of you who are fighting to survive a Depression and Monetary Collapse, we dedicate this message to you. Stay strong, stay positive, and never give up hope. Together, we can overcome anything and create a brighter future for ourselves and generations to come.

INTRODUCTION

Money has played an integral role in human society for thousands of years. From the earliest civilizations to the modern era, the concept of exchanging goods for a currency has been the cornerstone of economic activity. The earliest forms of money were simple objects such as shells or beads, which were used in bartering. However, the invention of coins in ancient Greece marked the beginning of the modern monetary system that we know today.

Despite the countless benefits of money, monetary collapse has been a recurring issue throughout history. A monetary collapse can lead to devastating effects on an economy, including hyperinflation and economic depression. Economic depression is a prolonged period of economic stagnation characterized by high unemployment and low productivity. It results from a decrease in the circulation of money, leading to a decline in economic activity.

One of the most notable examples of a

monetary collapse in modern times is the Great Depression of the 1930s. This catastrophic event was caused by the failure of the banking system, which resulted in the loss of people's savings and a decline in economic activity. The Great Depression led to the creation of central banks and the development of monetary policy tools to stabilize the economy and prevent future collapses.

Another example of a monetary collapse was the hyperinflation that occurred in Germany during the early 1920s. This was a time when the German Mark essentially became worthless, leading to widespread economic and social unrest. Some historians suggest that this may have been a contributing factor to Hitler's rise to power and the outbreak of World War II.

In recent times, countries such as Venezuela and Zimbabwe have experienced hyperinflation and monetary collapse, leading to widespread economic turmoil and social unrest. In such cases, individuals have had to resort to extreme measures, such as bartering, hoarding goods, or even using foreign currency to survive.

The history of money is a fascinating subject that has had a significant impact on human civilization. However, monetary collapse and depression have been significant challenges throughout history. We have learned from past mistakes and developed strategies to prevent them from happening again, but it is important to remain vigilant and take appropriate action to avoid economic collapse. By understanding the causes and effects of monetary collapse, individuals and governments can work together to ensure a stable and prosperous economic future.

The importance of
being prepared

The global economy is constantly in flux, and we have seen throughout history that monetary collapses and depressions can occur suddenly and without warning. It is essential to be prepared for such events, as they can have a devastating impact on individuals, families, and communities.

The first step in being prepared for a monetary collapse or depression is to understand what these terms mean. A monetary collapse occurs when the value of a currency rapidly decreases, resulting in hyperinflation and a loss of confidence in the currency. This can lead to a shortage of goods and services, widespread poverty, and economic turmoil. A monetary depression, on the other hand, is a prolonged period of economic stagnation, marked by high unemployment and low productivity. It results from a decrease in the circulation of money, leading to a decline in economic activity.

Now that we understand what a monetary collapse and depression are, let us examine why it is essential to be prepared for such events. Firstly, a monetary collapse or depression can result in the loss of savings, investments, and retirement funds. People who are not prepared may find themselves without financial resources to pay for basic needs such as food, shelter, and healthcare. Furthermore, a monetary collapse or depression can lead to social and political unrest, as people struggle to survive in a harsh economic climate. Being prepared can help individuals and families weather the storm and avoid the worst of the economic and social consequences.

So, how can one be prepared for a monetary collapse or depression? Expert recommendations include:

Diversify your investments: Instead of putting all your eggs in one basket, consider investing in a variety of assets such as stocks, bonds, real estate, and precious metals. This will help protect your assets in the event of a currency devaluation or economic downturn.

Build an emergency fund: Experts recommend having at least six months' worth of living expenses saved in an emergency fund. This will provide a financial cushion in case of a sudden job loss or another financial setback.

Learn practical skills: Being able to grow your food, fix your car, or perform basic home repairs can be incredibly useful during an economic crisis. Learning practical skills can help you save money and survive in a harsh economic climate.

Stock up on essentials: In the event of a monetary collapse or depression, goods, and services may become scarce. Stocking up on non-perishable food, water, and other essentials can help you and your family weather the storm.

Stay informed: Pay attention to economic indicators such as inflation rates, unemployment rates, and the value of your currency. Staying informed can help you make informed financial decisions and prepare for a possible economic downturn.

Being prepared for a monetary collapse or depression is crucial for anyone who wants to protect their financial well-being and ensure their family's survival. By following expert recommendations such as diversifying your investments, building an emergency fund, learning practical skills, stocking up on essentials, and staying informed, you can be ready for whatever economic challenges may come your way. Do not wait until it is too late - start preparing today.

I. UNDERSTANDING ECONOMIC DOWNTURNS

Bank failures have been a common occurrence throughout history and have been the cause of many monetary collapses and economic depressions.

One of the earliest recorded bank failures was the Panic of 1819 in the United States. A decrease in demand for American exports, which led to a decrease in the value of American currency, caused panic. Banks at the time were issuing banknotes more than their reserves, and when people started to redeem their notes for gold, the banks were unable to fulfill the demand. This led to a wave of bank failures and the depression that followed.

Another significant example of bank failures causing economic collapse was the Great Depression of the 1930s. Several factors caused the depression, including the stock market crash of 1929, but one of the main factors was the failure of the banking system. Banks at the time were lending money to people to invest in the stock market, and when the market crashed, various people were unable to repay their loans. This led to a wave of bank failures and a decline in economic activity.

The failure of banks during the Great Depression led to the creation of the Federal Deposit Insurance Corporation (FDIC) in the United States. The FDIC was established to insure deposits in the event of a bank failure and to prevent runs on banks. This was a significant step in preventing bank failures from causing economic collapse.

Another notable example of bank failures causing a monetary collapse was the hyperinflation that occurred in Germany during the early 1920s. This was a time when the German Mark essentially became worthless, leading to widespread economic and social unrest. The printing of too much money caused hyperinflation by the German government to pay for war reparations. The failure of banks to manage the circulation of currency and controlled to the collapse of the economy and the rise of the Nazi party.

The most recent example of bank failure causing an economic collapse is the 2008 financial crisis. Several factors caused the crisis, including the collapse of the housing market, but one of the main factors was the failure of the banking system. Banks at the time were issuing loans to people with poor credit, and when these loans started to default, banks were unable to cover their losses. This led to a wave of bank failures and a decline in economic activity.

In response to the 2008 financial crisis, governments around the world took steps to prevent future bank failures from causing economic collapse. One of the most significant steps was the implementation of accentuated tests for banks to ensure they had enough capital to withstand economic shocks. Stress tests have become a standard practice for banks and have helped prevent future bank failures from causing economic collapse.

Bank failures have been a significant cause of monetary collapses and economic depressions throughout history. The failure of banks to manage the circulation of currency, control inflation, and insure deposits has led to widespread economic instability. However, we have not learned from past mistakes even when taking steps to prevent bank failures from causing economic collapse. The creation of the FDIC, the implementation of stress tests, and the development of monetary policy tools have all tried to prevent bank failures from causing economic collapse, but measures have failed again. Governments, banks, and individuals need to remain vigilant and prepared for another economic shock that may occur. We're living in a time where world banks and countries are not stable when any day all can fall apart, affecting everyone on the planet.

Causes of economic downturns

An economic downturn is a period of significant economic decline, characterized by a decrease in economic activity and a rise in unemployment rates. Such downturns can have serious and long-lasting impacts on individuals, businesses, and entire economies. While the causes of economic downturns can be complex and multifaceted, several common factors contribute to their occurrence.

One of the primary causes of economic downturns is a decrease in consumer spending. Consumer spending is the engine that drives economic growth, as businesses rely on consumers to purchase their goods and services. When consumers are unable or unwilling to spend, businesses suffer, leading to decreased economic activity and a rise in unemployment rates. This can occur for a variety of reasons, including job losses, high levels of debt, and uncertainty about the future.

Another significant cause of economic downturns is a decrease in business investment. When businesses are not investing in new equipment, technology, or expansion, it can lead to a decline in economic activity. When businesses are faced with higher taxes or regulatory burdens, they can find it difficult and costly to invest in growth.

Monetary policy can also play a role in causing economic downturns. When central banks reduce the money supply or raise interest rates, it can lead to a decrease in consumer spending and business investment. This is because higher interest rates make it more expensive for businesses and individuals to borrow money, reducing their ability to invest and spend.

Another factor that can contribute to economic downturns is a decrease in exports. When countries experience a decline in exports, it can lead to decreased economic activity, as businesses are unable to sell their goods and services to foreign markets. This can occur due to a variety of factors, including changes in global trade policies or shifts in demand for certain products or services.

In addition to these factors, external shocks such as natural disasters, pandemics, or geopolitical events also cause economic downturns. These shocks can disrupt supply chains, reduce consumer confidence, and lead to significant economic decline.

Historically, bank failures have also

played a significant role in causing economic downturns. In the early 20th century, a series of bank failures led to the Great Depression, a period of economic decline that lasted for over a decade. The failure of banks can have a cascading effect on the economy, as it can lead to a decrease in the money supply and a rise in unemployment rates.

One example of a significant bank failure was the collapse of Lehman Brothers in 2008. The failure of Lehman Brothers, one of the largest investment banks in the United States, triggered a global financial crisis that resulted in a severe economic downturn. The collapse of Lehman Brothers and other financial institutions led to a decrease in the money supply, a rise in unemployment rates, and a decline in economic activity that lasted for several years.

Economic downturns can have serious and long-lasting impacts on individuals, businesses, and entire economies. While the causes of economic downturns can be complex and multifaceted, several common factors contribute to their occurrence. These factors include a decrease in consumer spending, a decrease in business investment, changes in monetary policy, a decrease in exports, and external shocks. In addition, historical examples such as bank failures have shown that the failure of financial institutions can have significant consequences for the economy. To prevent economic downturns, policymakers must be vigilant in monitoring these factors and taking appropriate action when necessary.

Signs of an impending recession

One of the primary signs of an impending recession is a decline in economic growth. This can be measured by looking at the Gross Domestic Product (GDP) of a country. GDP is the value of all goods and services produced within a country in a given period, usually a year. When the GDP growth rate slows down, it indicates that the economy is not expanding as fast as it was, which is a warning sign of an impending recession.

Another sign of an impending recession is a decrease in consumer spending. When consumers are worried about their financial future, they tend to save more and spend less. This decrease in spending can have a significant impact on the overall economy, as consumer spending accounts for a large portion of economic activity.

An increase in unemployment is also a sign of an impending recession. When companies are struggling to make a profit, they may need to cut costs, which can lead to layoffs. Companies struggling to make a profit may need to cut costs, leading to layoffs, which can be a warning sign of an impending recession.

A decline in the stock market is another sign of an impending recession. I often saw the stock market as a leading indicator of the economy, as it reflects investor confidence in the future of companies and the overall economy. A sustained decline in the stock market can indicate that investors are worried about the future of the economy and are preparing for a potential recession.

Other signs of an impending recession include a decrease in business investment, a decrease in international trade, and a decrease in real estate prices. Each of these factors can have a significant impact on the broader economy and indicate that a recession may be imminent.

Finally, a decline in GDP is another sign that we are in a recession. GDP measures the value of all goods and services produced within a country in a given period, usually a year. When GDP declines for two consecutive quarters, they considered it a technical recession.

Recognizing the signs of an impending recession and the signs that indicate we are in a recession is essential for individuals, businesses, and policymakers. By understanding these signs, we can take steps to prepare for the impact of a recession and implement policies that can help mitigate its effects. While recessions are a normal part of the economic cycle, being aware of the warning signs can help us minimize their impact and ensure a more stable economic future.

II. PREPARING FOR A DEPRESSION

Building a stockpile of essentials is a crucial part of preparing for any potential disaster or emergency. Whether it is a natural disaster, economic collapse, or societal breakdown, having a stockpile of essential items can help ensure your survival and that of your loved ones.

Primarily, having a stockpile of essentials can provide you with a sense of security and peace of mind. In times of crisis, when resources are scarce and supply chains are disrupted, having a reserve of necessary items can help you and your family stay fed, hydrated, and safe. It is important to note that building a stockpile should be done gradually over time, as trying to accumulate everything at once can be overwhelming and costly.

When building a stockpile, it is essential to consider the items that you and your family will need in the event of an emergency. These items should include food, water, medical supplies, and other necessities. For food, it is important to choose items that are non-perishable and can be stored for an extended period, such as canned goods, dried fruits and vegetables, and grains. You should also consider purchasing a water filtration system or stockpiling water purification tablets to ensure that you have access to clean drinking water in the event of a disaster.

In addition to food and water, it is important to have medical supplies on hand. This should include basic first aid supplies, such as bandages, antiseptic ointment, and pain relievers, as well as any prescription medications that you or your family members may require. It is also a good idea to include a basic medical guide or manual in your stockpile so that you can provide appropriate medical care if needed.

Other essential items to include in your stockpile may include hygiene products such as soap, toothpaste, and toilet paper, as well as warm clothing and bedding in case of power outages or cold temperatures. It is also a clever idea to have a supply of batteries, flashlights, and other sources of light in case of power outages.

When building a stockpile of essentials, it is important to rotate your supplies regularly to ensure that they remain fresh and usable. This means periodically checking expiration dates and replacing items as needed. It is also important to keep your stockpile organized and easily accessible so that you can quickly locate what you need in an emergency.

Building a stockpile of essentials is a critical aspect of being a survivalist. By taking the time to gradually accumulate necessary items such as food, water, medical supplies, and other essentials, you can help ensure your family's survival in the event of a disaster or emergency. Remember to rotate your supplies regularly, keep your stockpile organized, and be prepared for any situation that may arise.

Learning to live frugally

The current global economic climate is volatile, and it is impossible to predict when the next recession or depression will hit. Being prepared for such an event is crucial, and one of the ways to prepare is by learning to live frugally. Living frugally means being conscious of one's spending habits, making smart financial decisions, and prioritizing essentials.

The first step to living frugally is to assess one's expenses and identify areas where cost-cutting can occur. This can be done by tracking expenses for a few months and analyzing where most of the money is going. For example, if a sizable portion of the budget is being spent on dining out, one could try cooking meals at home instead. This not only saves money but also provides an opportunity to eat healthier.

Another way to live frugally is by reducing energy consumption. This can be achieved by making minor changes such as turning off lights when leaving a room, unplugging electronics when not in use, and using energy-efficient appliances. These changes not only save money on electricity bills but also reduce one's carbon footprint.

Shopping smart is another way to live frugally. It is important to shop around for the best deals and buy items in bulk when possible. Buying generic or store-brand products instead of name-brand items can also save a significant amount of money. Additionally, taking advantage of sales, discounts, and coupons can help to stretch one's budget further.

Living frugally also involves being creative and resourceful. For example, instead of buying new clothes, one could try thrift store shopping or even consider learning how to mend or alter clothes. Additionally, instead of buying new furniture, one could consider re-purposing old furniture or buying used items.

Another important aspect of living frugally to prepare for depression is building a stockpile of essentials. This means stocking up on non-perishable food items, toiletries, and household supplies. It is important to buy items in bulk and store them properly to ensure they last for a long time. This not only ensures that one has enough supplies to last during tough times but also allows one to take advantage of bulk discounts.

In addition to these practical tips, it is essential to adopt a frugal mindset. This means learning to differentiate between needs and wants and making conscious spending decisions. For example, instead of buying a new car, one could consider purchasing a reliable used car. Similarly, instead of going on an expensive vacation, one could plan a staycation or a low-cost trip.

Learning to live frugally is an essential aspect of preparing for depression in the 21st century. By being mindful of expenses, reducing energy consumption, shopping smart, being creative, building a stockpile of essentials, and adopting a frugal mindset, one can be better equipped to weather tough economic times. It is important to remember that being frugal does not mean sacrificing the quality of life, but rather finding creative ways to prioritize essentials while living within one's means.

Diversifying your income

In today's world, it is becoming increasingly important to diversify your income. With economic uncertainty and job insecurity, having multiple sources of income can help provide stability and financial security. Diversifying your income means earning money from different sources, which can include part-time jobs, freelancing, investing, and starting a side business.

One of the most significant benefits of diversifying your income is that it reduces your reliance on a single source of income. If you lose your job or your primary source of income, having other income streams can help you stay afloat financially. This is particularly important in times of economic downturns or recessions, where job loss is more common.

One way to diversify your income is through part-time work. Many people take on part-time jobs in addition to their full-time jobs, especially in industries like retail and hospitality. Part-time work can provide a steady stream of income that can help supplement your primary source of income.

Freelancing is another popular way to diversify your income. Freelancing involves offering your services on a contract basis to clients. This can include writing, graphic design, social media management, and more. Freelancing offers the flexibility to work on your schedule, and you can often set yours.

Investing is another way to diversify your income. While investing does carry some risk, it can provide a significant source of passive income. This can include investing in stocks, bonds, real estate, and other assets. Investing requires some knowledge and research, but with the right strategy, it can help you grow your wealth over time.

Starting a side business is also a great way to diversify your income. Many successful businesses start as side hustles and grow into full-time ventures. Starting a business can be challenging, but it can also be very rewarding. With the rise of e-commerce, starting an online business has become more accessible than ever.

In addition to these strategies, there are also many ways to diversify your income through the gig economy. This can include driving for ride-sharing services like Uber and Lyft, delivering food for services like DoorDash and

Grubhub, and even renting out your home on vacation rental platforms like Airbnb.

Learning to diversify your income requires some planning and effort, but the benefits can be significant. By having multiple streams of income, you can reduce your financial stress and increase your financial security. Diversifying your income can also provide opportunities for personal growth and development. By taking on new challenges and learning new skills, you can improve your earning potential and your overall quality of life.

Diversifying your income is essential in today's economy. With economic uncertainty and job insecurity, having multiple sources of income can help provide stability and financial security. Whether it is through part-time work, freelancing, investing, starting a side business, or participating in the gig economy, there are many ways to diversify your income. By taking steps to diversify your income, you can reduce your financial stress and increase your financial security, while also pursuing new opportunities for personal growth and development.

Developing new skills

Developing new skills is essential in today's ever-changing and competitive job market. In addition to improving your employability, learning new skills can also provide a sense of personal fulfillment and increase your earning potential. Moreover, in times of economic uncertainty, developing new skills can help you pivot to a new career or start a side hustle, providing a much-needed source of income.

One of the most in-demand skills in today's job market is digital literacy. As technology continues to advance, many jobs now require basic proficiency in digital tools such as spreadsheets, email, and social media. For those looking to take their digital skills to the next level, there are plenty of online courses and tutorials available for free or at a low cost. Learning to code, for example, can open many opportunities in the tech industry, which is one of the fastest-growing sectors in the economy.

Another valuable skill to learn is communication. Effective communication is essential in any workplace, whether you are working in customer service or management.

Improving your communication skills can help you become a better listener, resolve conflicts more effectively, and build stronger relationships with colleagues and clients.

With the rise of remote work, project management skills are also becoming increasingly important. Learning how to manage projects, delegate tasks, and stay organized can help you stand out as a valuable team member in any industry. There are many online courses and certifications available for project management, including the popular Project Management Professional (PMP) certification.

For those interested in starting their own business, learning marketing and sales skills can be critical to success. Whether you are selling a product or a service, understanding how to effectively market and sell to your target audience is essential. Learning how to create a marketing plan, use social media for business, and develop persuasive sales pitches can help you attract and retain customers.

In addition to these specific skills, many soft skills can help you succeed in any career. Time management, problem-solving, and adaptability are just a few examples of soft skills that are highly valued by employers. Developing these skills can help you become more efficient and productive at work and can also your overall quality of life.

Developing new skills is an important part of preparing for the future, especially in times of economic uncertainty. Learning digital literacy, communication, project management, marketing, sales, and soft skills can improve your employability, increase your earning potential, and provide a sense of personal fulfillment. With so many online courses and resources available, there has never been a better time to start learning.

Investing in gold and other precious metals

Investing in gold and other precious metals has been a popular strategy for centuries, and with good reason. Gold and other precious metals have been used as a form of currency and a store of value for thousands of years. They are durable, easily divisible, and have a high intrinsic value. But why is it so important to invest in gold and other precious metals today?

One of the main reasons to invest in gold and other precious metals is to protect your wealth. Precious metals have been shown to hold their value over time, even during periods of economic instability and inflation. This means that if the value of paper currency or other assets decreases, the value of gold and other precious metals can increase, providing a hedge against inflation and economic downturns.

Another reason to invest in gold and other precious metals is that they are not tied to any specific currency or economy. Unlike stocks, bonds, or real estate, gold and other precious metals are universal assets that are valued all over the world. This means that they can provide a level of diversification to your investment portfolio, reducing your overall risk and exposure to any one specific asset or economy.

In addition to protecting your wealth and providing diversification, investing in gold and other precious metals can also offer potential profit opportunities. The price of gold and other precious metals can fluctuate based on supply and demand, global economic conditions, and political factors. This means that if you buy at the right time and sell at the right time, you can potentially make a profit on your investment.

So, how can you invest in gold and other precious metals? There are a few different options. One option is to purchase physical gold or other precious metals, such as coins or bars. This allows you to own the asset outright and have it in your possession. However, storing and securing physical gold can be a challenge, and there may be additional costs associated with storage and insurance.

Another option is to invest in gold and other precious metals through an exchange-traded fund (ETF). ETFs are investment vehicles that track the price of an underlying asset or index. In the case of gold and other precious metals, ETFs typically hold physical metal or futures contracts that track the price of the metal. This allows you to invest in gold and other precious metals without having to physically own and store the metal.

Finally, there are also mutual funds and individual stocks that invest in gold and other precious metals. These options can offer exposure to the precious metals market through a managed investment portfolio, but they may also come with higher fees and expenses.

Investing in gold and other precious metals can be an important part of a diversified investment portfolio. Precious metals offer protection against economic downturns, inflation, and currency fluctuations, and can also provide potential profit opportunities. Whether you choose to invest in physical gold, ETFs, mutual funds, or individual stocks, it is important to do your research and understand the risks and potential rewards before making any investment decisions.

Connecting with your community

In times of crisis, such as a monetary collapse or economic depression, it is important to have a strong support system in place. Connecting with your community and church can provide a lifeline of support and resources that can be invaluable during difficult times.

Community connections can provide access to resources that may not be readily available otherwise. For example, during a monetary collapse, local farmers may become a more important source of food. Building relationships with local farmers and community members who have the skills and resources to survive in such situations can be a crucial step in preparing for a crisis.

Churches can also provide a valuable network of support during difficult times. Many churches have programs in place to help those in need, such as food banks, clothing drives, and emergency funds. In addition, churches often provide a sense of community and belonging, which can be essential for mental and emotional well-being during challenging times.

There are several ways to connect with your community and church. One way is to simply attend regular events and services. This can help you build relationships with other members and become more familiar with the resources available. You can also volunteer for community events and church programs, which can help you meet new people and make a positive impact in your community.

Another way to connect with your community and church is to participate in local events and organizations. Many communities have groups dedicated to community services, such as volunteer organizations, service clubs, and charitable organizations. Joining one of these groups can provide opportunities to give back to your community while also building valuable relationships.

Connecting with your community and church can also provide a sense of purpose and meaning during difficult times. Helping others and contributing to your community can give you a sense of control and empowerment, even in the face of a crisis.

In addition to providing support during a crisis, community and church connections can also help you prepare for potential difficulties.

For example, participating in community events can help you learn about local resources and emergency preparedness plans. Building relationships with community members who have the skills and resources to survive in a crisis can also be an important part of preparing for potential challenges.

Overall, connecting with your community and church can provide a lifeline of support and resources during difficult times. Building relationships with local farmers, community members, and church members can provide access to essential resources and skills, while also providing a sense of purpose and belonging. Taking steps to connect with your community and church can be a crucial part of preparing for a monetary collapse or economic depression.

III. COPING WITH DEPRESSION DURING A MONETARY DEPRESSION

Depression is a serious mental illness that affects millions of people worldwide. It can be caused by a variety of factors, including genetic predisposition, traumatic events, and chemical imbalances in the brain. However, when a monetary depression occurs, depression can become even more prevalent. The financial strain, uncertainty, and loss of stability can trigger or worsen symptoms of depression.

During a monetary depression, it is crucial to prioritize your mental health and find ways to cope with depression. Here are some tips for coping with depression during a monetary depression:

Seek professional help: If you are struggling with depression, do not be afraid to seek professional help. A therapist or counselor can provide you with the tools and support you need to manage your depression. They can also help you develop coping strategies for dealing with the stresses of a monetary depression.

Stay connected: It is essential to stay connected with friends and family during a monetary depression. Isolation can worsen depression, so try to reach out and maintain social connections. If you are feeling alone, consider joining a support group or online community.

Practice self-care: Self-care is essential for managing depression. This means taking care of your physical, emotional, and mental health. Be available for activities you enjoy, such as reading, exercise, or meditation. Get enough sleep, eat a balanced diet, and avoid drugs and alcohol.

Find meaning and purpose: During a monetary depression, it can be challenging to find meaning and purpose in life. However, it is crucial to identify what is most important to you and focus on it. This could mean spending time with family, pursuing a passion, or volunteering in your community.

Stay positive: A positive attitude can go a long

way in managing depression. Try to focus on the positive aspects of your life, such as your relationships, accomplishments, and strengths. Practice gratitude by keeping a journal of things you are thankful for each day.

In addition to these tips, it is important to remember that depression is a treatable illness. With the right support and treatment, you can manage your symptoms and improve your quality of life. If you are struggling with depression during a monetary depression, do not hesitate to seek help. Remember, you are not alone, and there is hope for recovery.

Coping with depression during a monetary depression can be challenging, but it is possible. By prioritizing your mental health, staying connected, practicing self-care, finding meaning and purpose, and staying positive, you can manage your symptoms and improve your overall well-being. Remember, seeking professional help is always an option, and there is no shame in reaching out for support. Together, we can overcome the challenges of a monetary depression and emerge stronger on the other side.

Mental health and resilience

Mental health and resilience are crucial during any challenging time, and this is especially true during a monetary collapse. The stress and uncertainty that come with a financial crisis can take a toll on our emotional well-being, and it's important to have strategies in place to cope with these difficulties.

One of the most important things to remember during a monetary collapse is to take care of yourself. This means prioritizing self-care activities such as exercise, meditation, and relaxation techniques. These activities can help to reduce stress and promote feelings of calm and relaxation, which can be especially helpful during times of uncertainty and economic hardship.

Another important factor in maintaining mental health and resilience during a monetary collapse is social support. Connecting with friends, family, and community resources can provide a sense of belonging and help combat feelings of isolation and hopelessness. Joining a support group or attending community events can be an excellent way to build social connections and receive support during difficult times.

It is also important to stay informed and educated about the state of the economy and any potential changes that may impact your financial situation. This can help to reduce feelings of uncertainty and anxiety, as well as prepare you to make informed decisions about your finances.

In addition to these strategies, it is important to be mindful of negative thought patterns and develop a positive mindset. This can be challenging during a time of economic hardship but focusing on the things that you can control and finding gratitude in small things can help to shift your mindset and improve your outlook.

Finally, seeking professional help if needed is always an important step in maintaining mental health and resilience. This may include working with a therapist or counselor, seeking support from a mental health hotline, or utilizing other resources such as medication or other treatments.

In summary, coping with a monetary collapse requires a multi-faceted approach that addresses both physical and emotional needs. By prioritizing self-care activities, building social connections, staying informed, cultivating a positive mindset, and seeking professional help when needed, it is possible to maintain mental health and resilience even during the most challenging times.

Staying motivated and positive

In the face of a monetary collapse, it can be challenging to stay motivated and positive. The uncertainty of the situation, the loss of financial stability, and the fear of the unknown can all take a toll on one's mental and emotional well-being. However, it is important to remember that even in difficult times, there is always hope and resilience.

One way to stay motivated and positive during a monetary collapse is to focus on the things that are within your control. While you may not be able to control the larger economic factors at play, you can control how you respond to them. Take stock of your resources and plan for how you can make the most of what you have. Consider developing new skills or pursuing new opportunities that can help you weather the storm.

Another key to staying motivated and positive during a monetary collapse is to cultivate a strong support network. Lean on family, friends, and community members for emotional support and practical assistance. Together, you can share resources and work collaboratively to overcome the challenges ahead.

It is also important to maintain a positive mindset and focus on the opportunities that a monetary collapse may present. While it may be difficult to see now, challenging times often provide opportunities for growth and transformation. Use this time to reflect on your values and goals and consider how you can align your life with them more fully.

Above all, remember that you are not alone. Many people are facing similar challenges, and by coming together and supporting one another, we can emerge from this difficult period stronger and more resilient than ever before. Stay motivated, stay positive, and keep moving forward.

Additionally, it is essential to maintain a healthy perspective and avoid falling into the trap of negative thinking. While it may be easy to focus on the negative aspects of a monetary collapse, dwelling on them can lead to feelings of hopelessness and despair. Instead, try to remain optimistic and focus on the things that are going well in your life. Celebrate small victories, express gratitude for what you have, and seek out moments of joy and happiness wherever you can find them.

Another helpful strategy for staying motivated

and positive during a monetary collapse is to stay informed about the situation, but not obsess over it. It can be easy to get caught up in the 24-hour news cycle and social media, which can be overwhelming and lead to feelings of anxiety and stress. Instead, limit your exposure to negative news and information, and focus on positive stories and uplifting messages.

Finally, remember that self-care is critical during times of crisis. Be available for activities that bring you joy and relaxation, such as reading, exercising, or spending time in nature. Practice mindfulness and meditation to reduce stress and increase your sense of inner calm. And do not forget to take care of your physical health by getting enough sleep, eating a healthy diet, and staying hydrated.

Staying motivated and positive during a monetary collapse can be a challenge, but it is possible with the right mindset and support network. Focus on the things that are within your control, cultivate a positive mindset, stay informed but avoid obsessing over negative news, and practice self-care. By doing so, you can emerge from this difficult time stronger, more resilient, and more hopeful for the future.

Dealing with job loss or reduced income

A monetary collapse can often lead to job loss or reduced income, which can be a major source of stress and anxiety. However, there are several options available to individuals who find themselves in this situation and need to make up for the loss of income.

One option is to consider taking on a part-time or freelance job in addition to your current employment. This can help supplement your income and provide some financial stability during uncertain times. Many online platforms allow you to find freelance work in a variety of fields, such as writing, graphic design, or programming.

Another option is to consider starting your own business or pursuing a side hustle. With the rise of e-commerce and online marketplaces, it is easier than ever to start a business from home or on a small scale. For example, you could start an online store selling products you make or curate or offer a service such as tutoring or personal training.

You may also want to consider exploring new

career paths or upgrading your skills to make yourself more marketable in your field. This could involve going back to school, taking online courses, or pursuing a certification or credential in your area of expertise. This investment in yourself and your skills could pay off in the long run and help you secure a more stable and lucrative job.

Finally, it is important to review your expenses and identify areas where you can cut back to make up for the loss of income. This may involve downsizing your home, reducing your transportation costs, or cutting back on discretionary spending. While these measures may be difficult or uncomfortable, they can help you weather the storm and emerge from the monetary collapse in a stronger financial position.

While job loss or reduced income can be a challenging aspect of a monetary collapse, there are many options available to individuals looking to make up for the loss of income. By being proactive, resourceful, and resilient, you can overcome these challenges and find new opportunities for financial stability and success.

Adjusting your lifestyle

A monetary collapse can have a significant impact on families, requiring them to adjust their lifestyle and financial practices to cope with the changing economic landscape. While these adjustments may be difficult, they are essential for maintaining financial stability and ensuring the well-being of your family.

The first step in adjusting your lifestyle and family to cope with a monetary collapse is to assess your current financial situation and develop a budget. This involves tracking your expenses and income and identifying areas where you can cut back. For example, you may need to reduce your entertainment or dining out expenses or find ways to save on household utilities such as water and electricity.

Another key step is to develop a plan for managing debt and credit. This may involve paying off high-interest credit cards or consolidating debt to lower interest rates. It is also important to avoid taking on new debt and to only use credit when it is necessary.

To further reduce expenses, families can consider adopting a more minimalist lifestyle.

This involves cutting back on unnecessary possessions and focusing on the things that truly matter. For example, you may choose to reduce your wardrobe, simplify your home decor, or downsize your living space.

It is also important to involve your family in the process of adjusting to the monetary collapse. This includes discussing the situation with your spouse or partner and involving children in age-appropriate conversations about the family's financial situation. This can help build a sense of shared responsibility and help everyone feel invested in the process of adjusting.

Finally, families can consider adopting new practices to generate income or reduce expenses. For example, you may consider starting a home-based business, taking on a side hustle, or finding ways to generate passive income through investments. You may also consider finding ways to save on household expenses, such as growing your food, using public transportation, or shopping secondhand.

Adjusting your lifestyle and family to cope with a monetary collapse is a challenging but necessary process. By developing a budget, managing debt and credit, adopting a minimalist lifestyle, involving your family, and exploring new practices to generate income or reduce expenses, you can weather the storm and emerge from the crisis stronger and more resilient than ever before.

Managing debt and expenses

Managing debt and expenses is an essential part of financial planning, especially during times of economic uncertainty. Whether you are dealing with job loss, reduced income, or simply looking to build financial stability, there are several strategies you can use to manage your debt and expenses effectively.

The first step in managing debt and expenses is to develop a budget. This involves tracking your income and expenses and identifying areas where you can cut back. For example, you may want to reduce your spending on dining out or entertainment or find ways to save on utilities such as water and electricity. By setting a realistic budget and sticking to it, you can avoid overspending and ensure that you have enough money to cover your necessary expenses.

Another important strategy for managing debt and expenses is to prioritize your debts. This involves identifying the debts with the highest interest rates and paying them off first. For example, you may want to focus on paying off credit card debt before tackling other debts such as student loans or mortgages. By prioritizing your debts in this way, you can save money on interest charges and reduce the total amount of debt you owe over time.

Consolidating debt is another strategy that can be effective for managing debt and expenses. This involves combining multiple debts into a single loan with a lower interest rate. For example, you may be able to consolidate your credit card debt into a single loan with a lower interest rate, which can make it easier to manage your debt and reduce your overall monthly payments.

In addition to managing debt, it is also important to look for ways to reduce expenses. This may involve finding ways to save on household expenses such as groceries, transportation, or entertainment. For example, you may want to shop for groceries at discount stores or buy in bulk to save money on food. You may also want to consider using public transportation or carpooling to save money on transportation costs.

Finally, it is important to develop good financial habits that can help you manage your debt and expenses over the long term. This may involve setting financial goals, regularly reviewing your budget and expenses, and seeking advice from financial professionals when necessary. By developing these habits, you can ensure that you are making informed financial decisions and taking steps to achieve your financial goals.

Managing debt and expenses is an essential part of financial planning, especially during times of economic uncertainty. By developing a budget, prioritizing debts, consolidating debt, reducing expenses, and developing good financial habits, you can achieve financial stability and build a solid foundation for your future.

IV. NAVIGATING A MONETARY COLLAPSE

Understanding hyperinflation and currency devaluation:

A monetary collapse can be a challenging time for individuals and businesses, as the economy experiences hyperinflation and currency devaluation. Understanding these concepts and navigating them effectively can be key to minimizing financial losses and maintaining financial stability.

Hyperinflation occurs when there is a rapid and excessive increase in the price of goods and services in a country. This is often caused by an increase in the money supply, which can lead to a devaluation of the currency. In a hyperinflationary environment, the cost of living can skyrocket, making it difficult for individuals and businesses to manage their expenses.

One way to navigate hyperinflation is to invest in assets that hold their value in times of inflation, such as gold or real estate. These assets can act as a hedge against inflation, providing a store of value that can help preserve wealth. Another strategy is to seek out investment opportunities that are likely to benefit from inflation, such as commodities or certain types of stocks.

Currency devaluation occurs when the value of a country's currency falls relative to other currencies. This can be caused by a variety of factors, including high inflation, economic instability, or political turmoil. In a devaluation scenario, the purchasing power of a currency can decline rapidly, making it more difficult to import goods and services.

One strategy for navigating currency devaluation is to diversify your holdings across multiple currencies. This can help spread your risk and reduce your exposure to a single currency. You may also want to consider investing in assets denominated in different currencies, such as stocks or bonds issued by foreign companies or governments.

Another strategy is to protect your savings by investing in assets that are likely to hold their value in a devaluation scenario. This may include assets such as gold or other precious metals, real estate, or certain types of commodities.

Navigating a monetary collapse can be a

challenging time for individuals and businesses, especially when facing hyperinflation and currency devaluation. By understanding these concepts and developing strategies to manage them, such as investing in assets that hold their value, diversifying your holdings, and protecting your savings, you can help minimize your financial losses and maintain financial stability during these challenging times.

Investing in foreign currencies and assets

Investing in foreign currencies and assets can be a smart strategy to protect your wealth during a monetary collapse. As the value of a domestic currency declines, investments denominated in foreign currencies can hold their value and provide a hedge against inflation.

One way to invest in foreign currencies is to buy and hold foreign currency deposits or bonds. This can help diversify your holdings and provide a hedge against domestic currency depreciation. For example, if you live in a country where the currency is expected to depreciate rapidly, you may want to consider investing in a currency such as Gold or silver, which is typically viewed as a haven currency.

Another way to invest in foreign currencies is through currency ETFs or mutual funds. These funds allow you to invest in a basket of currencies, providing diversification and potentially higher returns than individual currency holdings. For example, the WisdomTree Bloomberg US Dollar Bullish Fund is an ETF that invests in a basket of foreign currencies to provide exposure to a diversified portfolio of foreign exchange rates.

Investing in foreign assets is another strategy that can provide a hedge against domestic currency depreciation. This may include investing in foreign real estate, stocks, or bonds denominated in foreign currencies. For example, if you live in a country where the economy is expected to struggle during a monetary collapse, you may want to consider investing in foreign stocks or bonds in a more stable economy.

In addition to investing in foreign currencies and assets, it is also important to consider the risks associated with these investments. Investing in foreign currencies and assets can involve currency risk, political risk, and other factors that can impact investment returns. Therefore, it is important to carefully research and understand the risks before investing in foreign currencies and assets.

Investing in foreign currencies and assets can be an effective strategy to protect your wealth during a monetary collapse. By diversifying your holdings and investing in a variety of currencies and assets, you can potentially minimize your risk and maximize your returns. However, it is important to carefully research and understand the risks associated with these investments before investing. With the right strategy and approach, investing in foreign currencies and assets can help you navigate a monetary collapse and protect your financial future.

Bartering and trading goods and services

In times of economic crisis or monetary collapse, bartering and trading goods and services can be a valuable strategy for individuals and businesses to get by. Bartering involves exchanging goods or services directly with others without using money as a medium of exchange.

One of the benefits of bartering and trading goods and services is that it can provide access to goods and services that may not be available for purchase with cash. For example, during a monetary collapse, it may be difficult to obtain necessities like food and clothing due to a shortage of cash. However, through bartering and trading, individuals and businesses can exchange goods and services they have for those they need without the need for cash.

Another benefit of bartering and trading is that it can provide a way to generate income without relying on traditional sources of employment. For example, if you have a skill or talent such as cooking or carpentry, you can exchange your services for other goods or services you need. This can provide a source of income even in a tough economic environment.

In addition, bartering and trading can help build stronger communities by fostering relationships between individuals and businesses. When people exchange goods and services with each other, they build trust and cooperation, which can strengthen community ties and provide a support network in times of crisis.

However, bartering and trading also have their challenges. For example, it can be difficult to determine the value of goods and services in a bartering system. Additionally, it can be challenging to find individuals and businesses with whom to trade, especially if there is limited connectivity or transportation options.

To overcome these challenges, some individuals and businesses have turned to online bartering and trading platforms. These platforms allow users to connect with others and exchange goods and services in a more organized and efficient manner. Examples of these platforms include BarterOnly, Tradeaway, and U-Exchange.

Bartering and trading goods and services can be a valuable strategy for individuals and businesses to get by during a monetary collapse. By exchanging goods and services without the need for cash, individuals can access necessary goods and services and generate income in a tough economic environment. While there are challenges to bartering and trading, online platforms can provide a more efficient and organized way to connect with others and exchange goods and services.

Preparing for economic chaos

Preparing for economic chaos can be a daunting task, but individuals and businesses need to do so to minimize the impact of economic downturns or even a complete economic collapse.

Build an emergency fund: **One of the most important ways to prepare for economic chaos is to build an emergency fund. This fund should cover at least three to six months of living expenses and be easily accessible in case of an emergency. This can help individuals and businesses weather financial storms and avoid getting into debt.**

Diversify your income: **Having multiple streams of income can help individuals and businesses weather economic chaos. This could include starting a side business, investing in stocks or real estate, or taking on freelance work. By diversifying income sources, individuals and businesses can reduce their reliance on a single source of** income and be better prepared for economic shocks.

Reduce debt: Debt can be a major burden during economic chaos. Therefore, individuals and businesses should aim to reduce their debt as much as possible. This could include paying off credit card debt, student loans, and mortgages. Reducing debt can free up money to cover basic living expenses during tough economic times.

Invest in precious metals: precious metals like gold and silver have historically held their value during economic crises. Therefore, individuals and businesses could consider investing in these metals to protect their wealth during economic chaos.

Stockpile essentials: In times of economic chaos, necessities like food, water, and toiletries can become scarce. Therefore, individuals and businesses could consider stockpiling these essentials to ensure they have enough to get by during tough times.

Learn new skills: During economic chaos, certain skills become more valuable than others. Therefore, individuals and businesses could consider learning new skills that could be useful during tough economic times. For example, learning how to garden or fix cars could help individuals and businesses save money on essential items.

Stay informed: Staying informed about economic trends and developments can help individuals and businesses make informed decisions about their finances. This could include reading financial news, following economic indicators, and staying up to date on government policies that could affect the economy.

Preparing for economic chaos requires a combination of financial planning, diversification, and skill-building. By building an emergency fund, diversifying income sources, reducing debt, investing in precious metals, stockpiling essentials, learning new skills, and staying informed, individuals and businesses can be better prepared to weather economic downturns or even a complete economic collapse.

V. SUSTAINABLE LIVING DURING ECONOMIC DOWNTURNS

Sustainable living is a way of life that is designed to preserve the environment, support a healthy lifestyle, and contribute to a more equitable society. It involves making conscious choices about the resources we use, the products we consume, and the impact we have on the planet. Sustainable living is particularly important during an economic downturn because it can help us to weather the financial storm and build resilience for the future.

During an economic downturn, many people struggle to make ends meet. Jobs may be lost, wages may be cut, and the cost of living may rise. In such times, sustainable living can help us to reduce our expenses and live within our means. For example, we can reduce our energy bills by using energy-efficient appliances and turning off lights and electronics when they are not in use. We can also save money by reducing our water consumption, buying second-hand goods, and repairing items instead of throwing them away.

In addition to helping us save money, sustainable living can also help us to become more self-sufficient. By growing our food, for example, we can reduce our reliance on expensive grocery stores and support local agriculture. Similarly, by reducing our dependence on fossil fuels, we can build a more resilient energy system that is less vulnerable to price shocks and supply disruptions.

Sustainable living is also important for protecting the environment. During an economic downturn, there may be pressure to prioritize short-term economic gains over long-term environmental sustainability. However, the consequences of such decisions can be severe, leading to climate change, pollution, and other environmental problems. By living sustainably, we can reduce our impact on the planet and help to mitigate the effects of climate change.

Moreover, sustainable living can contribute to a more equitable society. During an economic downturn, vulnerable populations are often hit the hardest, including low-income families, people with disabilities, and communities of color. Sustainable living can help to address these inequities by promoting access to affordable housing, public transportation, and other necessities. It can also create opportunities for new jobs and industries in fields such as renewable energy, waste reduction, and sustainable agriculture.

, sustainable living is a crucial practice during an economic downturn. It can help us to reduce our expenses, become more self-sufficient, protect the environment, and build a more equitable society. By making conscious choices about the resources, we use and the impact we have on the planet, we can weather the financial storm and create a more sustainable and resilient future.

Strategies for reducing your carbon footprint

Reducing dependency on the world and living sustainably is essential for ensuring the long-term well-being of our planet and its inhabitants. Here are some strategies that can help individuals reduce their dependency on the world and live more sustainably.

Reduce Consumption: One of the most effective ways to reduce dependency on the world is to consume less. Individuals can start by reducing their consumption of energy, water, and other natural resources. This can be achieved by using energy-efficient appliances, taking shorter showers, turning off lights when not in use, and recycling.

Grow Your Food: Growing your own is an excellent way to reduce dependency on the world and live sustainably. It can also help to reduce the carbon footprint associated with the transportation and distribution of food. Individuals can start by growing their herbs and vegetables, either in a garden or in containers.

Use Renewable Energy: Using renewable energy sources such as solar or wind power can significantly reduce dependency on the world and live sustainably. Individuals can install solar panels on their rooftops or purchase energy from renewable sources.

Choose Sustainable Products: Choosing sustainable products is another way to reduce dependency on the world and live sustainably. Individuals can choose products made from renewable materials such as bamboo, recycled paper, or organic cotton. They can also choose products that are made locally, reducing the carbon footprint associated with transportation.

Reduce Waste: Reducing waste is an essential strategy for living sustainably. Individuals can start by reducing their use of single-use plastics, such as straws and plastic bags. They can also recycle, compost, and donate items they no longer need.

Support Sustainable Initiatives: Supporting

sustainable initiatives is an excellent way to reduce dependency on the world and live sustainably. Individuals can support local farmers' markets, community gardens, and environmental organizations. They can also advocate for policies that promote sustainability at the local, state, and national levels.

Reduce Transportation: Transportation is a significant source of greenhouse gas emissions, and reducing it is crucial for living sustainably. Individuals can start by walking or biking instead of driving, carpooling, using public transportation, or purchasing an electric or hybrid vehicle.

Reducing dependency on the world and living sustainably is essential for ensuring a healthy planet for future generations. Individuals can take small steps to reduce their consumption, grow their food, use renewable energy, choose sustainable products, reduce waste, support sustainable initiatives, and reduce transportation. By taking these steps, individuals can reduce their impact on the environment and contribute to a more sustainable future.

Developing self-sustaining practices, such as gardening and composting

Developing self-sustaining practices such as gardening and composting can help individuals reduce their environmental impact and contribute to a more sustainable future.

Gardening is an excellent way to develop self-sustaining practices. By growing your food, you reduce your dependence on industrial agriculture and the transportation of food, which can have a significant carbon footprint. Gardening can also promote healthy eating habits, as fresh fruits and vegetables are often more nutritious than processed foods.

There are many ways to garden, depending on your available space and resources. For example, container gardening is a great option for those with limited space. You can grow herbs, vegetables, and fruits in pots on a balcony, patio, or windowsill. Raised bed gardening is another option that allows for more significant yields and can be customized to fit your needs. You can also consider community gardening, which involves sharing garden plots with others in your community.

Composting is another self-sustaining practice that can reduce waste and improve soil health. Composting involves the natural decomposition of organic materials, such as food scraps, yard waste, and paper products, into a nutrient-rich soil amendment. Composting can reduce the amount of organic material that ends up in landfills, which contributes to greenhouse gas emissions.

There are many different methods of composting, including indoor composting, outdoor composting, and vermicomposting. Indoor composting involves using a compost bin or worm bin to break down food scraps and other organic materials inside your home. Outdoor composting involves using a compost bin or pile in your yard, while vermicomposting involves using worms to break down food scraps and other organic materials.

Practical examples of self-sustaining practices can be seen in many communities around the world. For example, the city of San Francisco has implemented a mandatory composting program that requires residents to separate food scraps and yard waste from regular garbage. The compost is then used to fertilize local gardens and farms. In New York City, urban farming initiatives have transformed vacant lots and rooftops into thriving gardens that produce fresh fruits and vegetables for local communities.

Developing self-sustaining practices such as gardening and composting can have many benefits for individuals and communities. By growing your food and composting, you can reduce your environmental impact and contribute to a more sustainable future. Practical examples of self-sustaining practices can be seen in communities around the world, demonstrating the feasibility and importance of these practices.

Using renewable energy sources, such as solar panels and wind turbines

As the world becomes more aware of the impact of fossil fuels on the environment, the use of renewable energy sources, such as solar panels and wind turbines, is becoming increasingly popular.

Renewable energy sources have many advantages over traditional fossil fuels. One of the most significant benefits is that they do not produce harmful emissions, such as greenhouse gases, which contribute to climate change. Additionally, renewable energy sources are often more cost-effective than fossil fuels in the long term, as the cost of production and installation continues to decrease.

Solar panels are one of the most popular forms of renewable energy. They work by converting the energy from the sun into electricity. Solar panels are made up of photovoltaic cells that are arranged in a grid-like pattern. When sunlight hits the cells, it creates an electric field that generates a flow of electricity. This electricity can be used to power homes, businesses, and even entire cities.

One of the benefits of solar panels is that they are low maintenance and can last for decades. Additionally, they can be installed on rooftops, which means that they do not take up any additional space. However, the cost of installation can be high, and solar panels may not be suitable for all areas, as they require direct sunlight to function.

Wind turbines are another form of renewable energy. They work by harnessing the power of the wind to generate electricity. Wind turbines have large blades that spin when the wind blows, which creates rotational energy that is converted into electricity. Like solar panels, wind turbines can be used to power homes, businesses, and cities.

One of the benefits of wind turbines is that they have a relatively small footprint and can be installed on both land and sea. Additionally, wind energy is often cheaper than other forms of renewable energy, and the cost of production and installation continues to decrease. However, wind turbines can be noisy and may have an impact on local wildlife, such as birds.

Using renewable energy sources such as solar panels and wind turbines has many benefits for the environment and society. By reducing our reliance on fossil fuels, we can reduce harmful emissions and contribute to a more sustainable future. Solar panels and wind turbines are two popular forms of renewable energy that are increasingly being used around the world. While there are some limitations to these technologies, they represent an important step towards a more sustainable and equitable energy system.

Reducing waste and adopting a minimalistic lifestyle

One of the most significant benefits of reducing waste is that it can save money. By using fewer disposable products and choosing products with minimal packaging, individuals can reduce their expenses and stretch their resources further. Additionally, reducing waste can help protect the environment by minimizing the amount of waste that ends up in landfills, which contributes to greenhouse gas emissions and other environmental problems.

There are many ways to reduce waste, including using reusable containers for food and beverages, buying products in bulk, and composting food scraps and yard waste. By adopting these practices, individuals can significantly reduce the amount of waste they produce and save money in the process.

Another important practice for navigating a monetary collapse is adopting a minimalistic lifestyle. Minimalism involves simplifying one's life by getting rid of unnecessary possessions and focusing on what is truly important. By adopting a lifestyle, individuals can reduce their expenses and free up resources for the most essential needs, such as food, shelter, and healthcare.

There are many ways to adopt a minimalist lifestyle, including decluttering possessions, avoiding impulse purchases, and focusing on experiences rather than material possessions. By embracing minimalism, individuals can learn to live with less and find greater fulfillment in life's simple pleasures.

We can see practical examples of reducing waste and adopting a minimalist lifestyle in sufficient communities around the world. For example, the zero-waste movement encourages individuals to reduce their waste by using reusable containers, composting, and buying products in bulk. The tiny house movement promotes minimalistic living by encouraging individuals to live in small, affordable homes that are often constructed using sustainable materials.

Reducing waste and adopting a minimalist lifestyle are two important practices for navigating a monetary collapse. By reducing waste and simplifying one's life, individuals can save money and free up resources for more essential needs. We can see practical examples of these practices in communities around the world, demonstrating the feasibility and importance of reducing waste and adopting a minimalistic lifestyle.

VI. BUILDING A COMMUNITY RESILIENT TO ECONOMIC DOWNTURNS

Community resilience is an essential component of surviving and thriving during economic downturns. In times of financial crisis, communities that come together and support one another are more likely to weather the storm and emerge stronger.

The first reason community resilience is important during economic downturns is that it can provide a safety net for individuals and families. When times are tough, it can be difficult for individuals to make ends meet, pay bills, and put food on the table. However, when communities come together, they can provide support, resources, and a sense of belonging that can help individuals through difficult times.

One way that communities can build resilience is by establishing mutual aid networks. Mutual aid networks are groups of individuals who come together to share resources, skills, and support during times of crisis. These networks can provide everything from food and shelter to medical care and emotional support. By establishing mutual aid networks, communities can create a safety net that can help individuals and families through difficult times.

Another important aspect of community resilience is the ability to adapt to changing circumstances. When economic downturns occur, communities that can adapt to the changing economic landscape are more likely to thrive. This can involve everything from finding new sources of income to reimagining local economies and creating new businesses.

One example of a community that has successfully adapted to changing circumstances is the city of Detroit. After the collapse of the auto industry, Detroit faced significant economic challenges. However, rather than giving up, the community came together to create new businesses, promote urban farming, and build a more sustainable local economy. Today, Detroit is a thriving city that has bounced back from economic hardship.

Community resilience is an essential component of surviving and thriving during economic downturns. By coming together, establishing mutual aid networks, and adapting to changing circumstances, communities can provide a safety net for individuals and families, promote economic growth, and emerge stronger from difficult times. As we navigate the challenges of the current economic landscape, it is more important than ever to build and support resilient communities.

Developing a support network of friends, family, and neighbors

Developing a support network of friends, family, and neighbors is essential for maintaining well-being and navigating difficult times. When we have a strong support network, we have a group of people who can offer emotional support, practical assistance, and a sense of community.

One of the main benefits of developing a support network is that it can provide emotional support during challenging times. When we are going through difficult situations, it can be helpful to have someone to talk to who can offer empathy, encouragement, and a listening ear. This can be particularly important during times of financial hardship, job loss, or other stressful events.

Another important benefit of a support network is the practical assistance it can provide. For example, neighbors can help with childcare, transportation, or household tasks, while family members and friends can provide financial assistance or help with job searches. When we have a support network in place, we have a group of people who can offer practical assistance when we need it most.

Building and maintaining a support network can involve a variety of strategies. One important strategy is to reach out to friends, family, and neighbors regularly. This can involve making phone calls, sending emails or texts, or arranging in-person visits. By staying in touch with our support network, we can build and maintain strong relationships that provide support when we need it most.

Another strategy for building a support network is to participate in community activities or events. This can include attending local events, joining community groups or clubs, or volunteering in the community. By participating in community activities, we can build connections with others who share our interests and values and develop a sense of belonging in our community.

Practical examples of developing a support network can be seen in many communities around the world. For example, in rural areas, neighbors may come together to form a "barn raising" to help a family build a new barn. In urban areas, neighbors may form a "black watch" to help keep their neighborhood safe. And in many communities, families, and friends come together to celebrate holidays and other special occasions, providing emotional support and a sense of community.

Developing a support network of friends, family, and neighbors is essential for maintaining well-being and navigating difficult times. By building and maintaining strong relationships, we can provide emotional support, practical assistance, and a sense of community when we need it most. Practical examples of developing a support network can be seen in communities around the world, demonstrating the importance and feasibility of this practice.

Strategies for building community resilience

Building community resilience is essential for creating sustainable and self-sufficient communities that can weather economic, environmental, and social challenges. Strategies for building community resilience can include forming local food co-ops, skill-sharing networks, and other initiatives that promote community building and resource sharing.

One strategy for building community resilience is to form local food co-ops. These co-ops can be used to purchase food in bulk, reducing costs and promoting healthy, locally sourced food. They can also be used to connect local farmers with consumers, creating a more sustainable and resilient food system. Food co-ops can also serve as a gathering place for community members to share recipes, cooking tips, and other food-related knowledge. For example, the Park Slope Food Coop in Brooklyn, New York, has been operating for over 40 years and has over 17,000 members who work together to provide affordable, healthy, and sustainable food to their community.

Another strategy for building community resilience is to create skill-sharing networks. These networks can be used to connect community members with a variety of skills and knowledge, allowing them to share resources and expertise. For example, a group of neighbors in a suburban area might form a network where they share tools, such as lawnmowers or gardening equipment, or they might offer to help each other with home repairs or other tasks. In some communities, skill-sharing networks have also been used to create community-led workshops, where members can learn new skills from each other. One such example is the Common Ground Health Clinic in New Orleans, which provides health care services, wellness education, and other support to low-income and uninsured community members.

Community gardens are another effective strategy for building community resilience. These gardens can be used to promote healthy eating, community building, and environmental sustainability. They can also be used to generate income and provide food for families in need. For example, the Garden of Hope in Hartford, Connecticut, is a community garden that provides fresh produce for local food pantries and serves as a gathering place for community members.

Lastly, community-based renewable energy initiatives can also be effective in building community resilience. These initiatives can involve the installation of solar panels or other renewable energy sources that provide energy for the community. They can also involve creating community-owned energy systems that are more sustainable and self-sufficient. For example, the Waverley Community Solar Project in Australia is a community-led initiative that has installed over 5,000 solar panels on the roofs of local businesses and homes, providing clean and sustainable energy to the community.

Strategies for building community resilience are essential for creating sustainable and self-sufficient communities. Initiatives such as local food co-ops, skill-sharing networks, community gardens, and community-based renewable energy projects can promote community building and resource sharing, while also promoting environmental sustainability and economic resilience. Practical examples of these initiatives can be seen in communities around the world, demonstrating their feasibility and effectiveness in building community resilience.

Developing alternative economic systems

Developing alternative economic systems is an important strategy for creating more sustainable and resilient communities. These systems can include local currencies, bartering networks, and other forms of exchange that prioritize local resources, reduce reliance on global markets, and promote community building.

One alternative economic system that has gained popularity in recent years is the use of local currencies. Local currencies are community-based systems of exchange that allow people to trade goods and services without relying on global currencies. These currencies can be used to support local businesses, promote community building, and reduce reliance on global financial systems. For example, the Brixton Pound in London, UK, is a local currency that can be used at over two hundred local businesses, promoting economic activity in the community, and supporting small businesses.

Another alternative economic system is bartering networks. Bartering is the exchange of goods or services without the use of money. Bartering networks can be used to connect community members who have goods or services to offer with those who need them, creating a more self-sufficient and sustainable community. For example, the Freecycle Network is a global network of local groups where people can offer or receive free items, promoting reuse and reducing waste.

Sharing economies is another example of alternative economic systems. Sharing economies are based on the idea of sharing resources and assets, rather than owning them. This can include sharing tools, cars, or even housing. Sharing economies can reduce resource consumption, promote community building, and create more equitable access to resources. For example, the car-sharing platform, Zipcar, allows members to rent cars by the hour, reducing the need for individual car ownership and promoting more sustainable transportation options.

Finally, worker-owned cooperatives are another alternative economic system that can promote community resilience. Worker-owned cooperatives are businesses that are owned and operated by their employees, with profits being distributed among the workers. This can create more equitable economic systems, promote community building, and reduce the negative impacts of globalization. For example, the Evergreen Cooperatives in Cleveland, Ohio, is a network of worker-owned cooperatives that provide employment and training opportunities to low-income residents, promoting economic self-sufficiency and community resilience.

Developing alternative economic systems is an important strategy for creating more sustainable and resilient communities. These systems can include local currencies, bartering networks, sharing economies, and worker-owned cooperatives, among others. Practical examples of these alternative economic systems can be seen in communities around the world, demonstrating their feasibility and effectiveness in promoting economic resilience and community building.

Advocating for policies that promote economic resilience

Advocating for policies that promote economic resilience is crucial in ensuring a sustainable and equitable future for our communities. These policies can range from investments in renewable energy to supporting small businesses, and they play a critical role in promoting community resilience, reducing reliance on global markets, and mitigating the impacts of economic downturns.

Investing in renewable energy is one policy that can promote economic resilience. Renewable energy sources, such as solar, wind, and geothermal power, can create jobs, reduce reliance on fossil fuels, and promote energy independence. Governments can promote the development of renewable energy by providing tax incentives for renewable energy projects, investing in research and development, and implementing policies that encourage the adoption of renewable energy sources. For example, Germany's "Energiewende" policy promotes the use of renewable energy sources and has helped the country become a leader in clean energy technology and job creation.

Another policy that can promote economic resilience is supporting small businesses. Small businesses are the backbone of many communities, providing jobs and contributing to local economies. Governments can support small businesses by providing financial incentives, reducing regulations, and investing in infrastructure that supports small business growth. For example, the city of Portland, Oregon, has implemented a program called "Shop Small PDX," which encourages residents to support local businesses and has provided over $2 million in grants and loans to small businesses affected by the COVID-19 pandemic.

In addition to these policies, there are other ways to promote economic resilience. For example, investing in education and job training programs can help create a more skilled workforce that is better equipped to navigate economic challenges. Governments can also promote equitable access to healthcare, housing, and other basic needs, which can reduce economic vulnerability and promote social cohesion.

Advocating for policies that promote economic resilience requires collective action and political will. Communities must come together to demand these policies from their elected representatives, and organizations must advocate for these policies at the local, state, and national levels. Examples of successful advocacy campaigns include the movement for a Green New Deal, which seeks to promote a just transition to renewable energy, and the Main Street Alliance, which advocates for policies that support small businesses.

Advocating for policies that promote economic resilience is crucial in ensuring a sustainable and equitable future for our communities. Examples of such policies include investing in renewable energy, supporting small businesses, and promoting access to education and basic needs. Achieving these policies requires collective action and political will, but the benefits are numerous, including job creation, reduced reliance on global markets, and increased community resilience in the face of economic downturns.

CONCLUSION

In today's unpredictable economic climate, the idea of a monetary crash or depression is no longer a distant possibility. It is a stark reality that we may have to face at some point in the future. However, it is important to remember that there are strategies that can be implemented to not only survive but also thrive during such a crisis.

The strategies outlined in this book, including developing self-sustaining practices, building community resilience, reducing waste, adopting a minimalistic lifestyle, using renewable energy sources, and advocating for policies that promote economic resilience, all hold tremendous potential in mitigating the impacts of economic downturns.

By taking a proactive approach to these strategies, individuals and communities can build a more sustainable and resilient future for themselves and future generations. It requires commitment, dedication, and a willingness to make positive changes in our lives and communities. But by doing so, we can not only weather the storm of economic uncertainty but also emerge stronger and more prepared for any future challenges that may come our way.

As we move forward, let us remember that we have the power to shape our economic future and that every action we take toward sustainability and resilience is a step in the right direction. With determination, creativity, and a shared vision for a better world, we can build a future that is not only economically secure but also environmentally and socially sustainable.

ENCOURAGEMENT

In times of depression and monetary collapse, it can be easy to feel overwhelmed and helpless. The economic challenges we face can seem insurmountable, leaving us feeling powerless and defeated. However, it is important to remember that we are not alone and that there are steps we can take to overcome these challenges and emerge stronger than ever before.

First and foremost, it is important to act. We cannot simply sit back and wait for the economy to improve on its own. Instead, we must be proactive in identifying areas where we can make a difference and take action to address them. This could include reducing our consumption and waste, supporting local businesses, or advocating for policies that promote economic resilience and sustainability.

We must also remember that we are not alone in this struggle. We are part of a larger community that is all affected by the same economic challenges. By working together, we can pool our resources, share our knowledge and expertise, and support one another through these tough times. This could include forming local food co-ops or skill-sharing networks, developing community gardens, and composting programs, or simply reaching out to friends and neighbors to offer support and encouragement.

Above all, it is important to maintain a positive attitude and outlook. Depression and monetary collapse can be incredibly challenging, but they also present opportunities for growth and change. By embracing this challenge and taking action to overcome it, we can emerge stronger and more resilient than ever before.

While depression and monetary collapse can be daunting, it is important to remember that we are not powerless. By acting, working together, and maintaining a positive attitude, we can overcome these challenges and emerge stronger and more resilient than ever before. Let us not be defeated by these challenges, but rather let us rise to meet them head-on, with determination, creativity, and a shared vision for a better world.

LAST THOUGHTS ON SURVIVAL DURING TOUGH TIMES

The world we live in is full of uncertainty, and we may face tough times at some point in our lives. Whether it is a natural disaster, economic downturn, or a personal crisis, the key to survival lies in being prepared and having the right mindset.

To start with, it is essential to develop self-sustaining practices, such as gardening and composting, to reduce our dependence on the world around us. By becoming more self-sufficient, we can weather the storm of any crisis that comes our way. We must also reduce our waste and adopt a minimalistic lifestyle to be more efficient with our resources.

Building community resilience is another critical factor in survival during tough times. We must form support networks of friends, family, and neighbors, and work together to share resources and knowledge. By building stronger and more interconnected communities, we can develop more significant resilience and face any challenge with more significant strength.

Moreover, using renewable energy sources such as solar panels and wind turbines can help us be less reliant on traditional energy sources, such as oil and coal. In addition, by advocating for policies that promote economic resilience and investing in renewable energy, we can create a sustainable future for generations to come.

We must keep in mind that tough times do not last forever. However, it is up to us to develop the right mindset and take proactive measures to survive and emerge stronger. By focusing on developing self-sustaining practices, building community resilience, using renewable energy sources, and advocating for policies that promote economic resilience, we can create a brighter future for ourselves and those around us.

As we navigate through tough times, let us remember the words of Helen Keller, who said, "Although the world is full of suffering, it is also full of overcoming it." So let us act, stay positive, and work together to overcome any challenges that come our way.

ACKNOWLEDGMENT

To all those who have dedicated their time, energy, and expertise to develop strategies for surviving a Depression and Monetary Collapse, and to all those who are currently facing tough times and wondering when it will end, this acknowledgment is for you.

Firstly, we acknowledge the resilience and strength of those who have faced adversity and continue to fight for a better future. Your determination, creativity, and compassion are an inspiration to us all.

We also acknowledge the vital role played by researchers, activists, and policymakers who work tirelessly to promote sustainable living, community resilience, and economic stability. Your knowledge, research, and advocacy have helped to shape the strategies that will enable us to navigate these challenging times.

Furthermore, we acknowledge the importance of communities coming together to support each other and develop strategies for survival.

Whether it is through building local food co-ops, sharing skills, or simply offering a helping hand to those in need, your efforts have made a real difference.

Finally, we acknowledge the difficult journey that many are currently facing. We understand the frustration, fear, and uncertainty that can arise during tough times, and we want you to know that you are not alone. There are people and resources available to help you through this challenging period.

In conclusion, we acknowledge the efforts of all those who have contributed to the development of strategies for surviving a Depression and Monetary Collapse, and we acknowledge the strength and resilience of those who are currently facing tough times. Together, we can navigate these challenges and emerge stronger and more resilient than ever before.

www.ingramcontent.com/pod-product-compliance
Lightning Source LLC
Chambersburg PA
CBHW070748220526
45467CB00018B/1309